Eight Dates
Essential Conversations for a Lifetime of Love

THE WORKBOOK

Copyright © 2023 by GuideGuru Publishing

All rights reserved. No part of this publication may be reproduced, distributed, or transmitted in any form or by any means, including photocopying, recording, or other electronic or mechanical methods, without the prior written permission of the publisher, except in the case of brief quotations embodied in critical reviews and certain other noncommercial uses permitted by copyright law. For permission requests, write to the publisher at the address below.

Disclaimer:

The information provided in this workbook is for general informational purposes only and should not be considered professional advice. While efforts have been made to ensure accuracy, we make no warranties regarding the completeness, accuracy, reliability, or availability of the content. The concepts discussed may not be applicable to every situation, and we recommend seeking professional advice for specific concerns. We are not liable for any loss or damage resulting from the use of this workbook. Please note that the information is current as of September 2021, and it is advisable to consult updated sources for the most current information. By using this workbook, you acknowledge and accept this disclaimer.

Thank you for choosing to engage with this book. We hope it helps you build a healthy and loving relationship with your partner.

LESSONS IN THIS WORKBOOK:

1. Lean on Me

2. Agree to Disagree

3. Let's Get It On

4. What's Your Number?

5. The Writing on the Wall

6. Room to Grow

7. After the Honeymoon

8. Let Love Rule

Chapter 1: Lean on Me

Lesson 1:

Reflecting on Friendship and Support

Write a journal entry describing the qualities and values that are important to you in a friendship. Reflect on how these qualities can contribute to building a strong foundation in a romantic relationship.

Write a letter to your partner expressing gratitude for their support and friendship. Describe specific instances where they have been there for you and how it has impacted your relationship. Reflect on the importance of this support in cultivating a healthy and fulfilling partnership.

_____
_____
_____
_____
_____
_____
_____
_____
_____
_____
_____
_____
_____
_____
_____
_____
_____
_____
_____
_____
_____
_____
_____
_____
_____
_____
_____
_____
_____
_____

Reflect on a challenging experience you and your partner have faced together. Write about how you supported each other during that time and how it strengthened your bond. Reflect on the lessons learned from that experience and how it can guide your future actions as a couple.

Lesson 2:

Cultivating Emotional Intimacy and Trust

Take turns with your partner and write down three vulnerable feelings or experiences that you haven't shared before. Share these writings with each other, focusing on creating a safe and non-judgmental space to discuss your emotions. Reflect on how this exercise deepens emotional intimacy and trust between you.

Write a list of actions or behaviors that contribute to building trust in a relationship. Reflect on how you and your partner can implement these actions and discuss them together. Consider any areas where trust may need to be strengthened and identify strategies for doing so.

Write a reflection on a time when you had to trust your partner or when they had to trust you. Describe the situation, the emotions involved, and the outcome. Reflect on how trust played a role in resolving the situation and strengthening your relationship.

Lesson 3:

Sharing Dreams and Establishing Rituals

Take some time individually to write down your personal dreams, goals, and aspirations. Then, come together with your partner and share these writings with each other. Discuss how you can support each other in achieving these dreams and establish a shared vision for your future as a couple.

Write a letter to your future selves as a couple, describing the life you envision together and the goals you hope to achieve. Reflect on how this exercise helps create a sense of shared purpose and motivation for your relationship.

Create a list of rituals of connection that you would like to establish in your relationship. These could be daily, weekly, or monthly activities that allow you to connect and show appreciation for each other. Reflect on the impact of these rituals on your relationship and how they contribute to relationship satisfaction.

Chapter 2: Agree to Disagree

Lesson 1:

Reflecting on Conflict and Disagreements

Write a journal entry reflecting on your past experiences with conflict in your relationship. Identify patterns or recurring themes in the disagreements you have had. Reflect on how you typically respond to conflict and how it impacts the overall health of your relationship.

Think of a recent disagreement you had with your partner. Write down your perspective and feelings about the issue. Then, try to put yourself in your partner's shoes and write down their perspective. Reflect on the similarities and differences between your viewpoints and how understanding each other's perspectives can foster empathy and respectful communication.

Write a letter to your partner expressing your commitment to finding "win-win" solutions in your disagreements. Share your desire to find compromises that satisfy both partners and create a sense of fairness and mutual respect. Reflect on how this approach can contribute to a healthier and more satisfying relationship.

Lesson 2:

Building Acceptance and Tolerance

Take turns with your partner and write down three qualities or characteristics that you appreciate and accept about them, even if they are different from your own. Share these writings with each other and discuss how acceptance and tolerance contribute to a positive relationship.

Write a reflection on a time when you and your partner had differing opinions or beliefs. Describe how you approached the situation and how you respected and explored each other's differences. Reflect on how building a culture of acceptance and tolerance has created an environment where differences can be embraced and respected.

Write a list of phrases or statements that you can use during conflicts to express your willingness to understand and accept your partner's perspective. Reflect on how using these phrases can promote open and respectful communication during disagreements.

Lesson 3:

Developing Conflict Resolution Skills

Practice active listening with your partner during a conversation. Write down the key points they make and the emotions they express. Reflect on your listening skills and identify areas for improvement, such as minimizing distractions or focusing on understanding rather than formulating a response.

Choose a specific conflict scenario you have experienced in your relationship. Write down three possible solutions or compromises that could satisfy both partners. Reflect on the potential benefits and drawbacks of each solution. Discuss these options with your partner and work together to find the most suitable resolution.

Write a letter to your future self, describing the conflict resolution skills you would like to develop or enhance. Reflect on specific behaviors or approaches you can practice to express needs and concerns constructively during conflicts. Consider how developing these skills can lead to healthier and more satisfying relationships.

Chapter 3: Let's Get It On

Lesson 1:

Reflecting on Sexual Intimacy

Write a journal entry reflecting on your own beliefs and attitudes towards sexual intimacy. Explore any personal values or experiences that may influence your views. Reflect on how these beliefs impact your communication and connection with your partner.

Write a letter to your partner expressing your appreciation for their sexual desires and needs. Share your commitment to open and honest communication about your own desires, boundaries, and expectations. Reflect on how this level of communication can promote a sense of safety and connection in the bedroom.

Reflect on a time when you and your partner successfully explored a new sexual experience or fulfilled a fantasy together. Write about the emotions and connection you felt during that experience. Reflect on how this exploration enhanced your sexual satisfaction and deepened emotional intimacy.

Lesson 2:

Discussing Desires, Boundaries, and Expectations

Create a list of sexual desires, boundaries, and expectations that you would like to discuss with your partner. Take turns sharing and discussing these lists, focusing on creating a safe and non-judgmental space for open communication. Reflect on how this exercise promotes understanding and connection in the bedroom.

Write a reflection on any challenges or discrepancies in sexual desire that you and your partner may have experienced. Describe the impact of these challenges on your relationship and emotional well-being. Brainstorm potential strategies and solutions for addressing these issues and creating a more satisfying sexual relationship.

Write a letter to your future self, describing the importance of prioritizing emotional and physical intimacy outside of the bedroom. Reflect on specific actions or behaviors you can implement to nurture this intimacy in your relationship. Consider how these efforts can contribute to a more satisfying and connected sexual relationship.

Lesson 3:

Experimenting and Prioritizing Intimacy

Take turns with your partner and write down three sexual fantasies or preferences that you would like to explore together. Share these writings with each other, focusing on creating a safe and adventurous space for open communication. Reflect on how exploring these fantasies and preferences can enhance your sexual satisfaction and deepen emotional intimacy.

Create a "sexual bucket list" with your partner, consisting of new experiences or activities you would like to try together. Reflect on the potential benefits of stepping outside of your comfort zone and how it can contribute to a more exciting and fulfilling sexual relationship.

Write a reflection on the role of emotional intimacy in your sexual relationship. Describe specific actions or behaviors that you can implement to nurture emotional connection and intimacy outside of the bedroom. Reflect on how prioritizing emotional and physical intimacy can enhance your overall satisfaction and connection as a couple.

Chapter 4: What's Your Number?

Lesson 1:

Reflecting on Financial Compatibility and Goals

Write a journal entry reflecting on your own financial values, attitudes, and goals. Consider your spending habits, saving preferences, and long-term financial aspirations. Reflect on how these factors may impact your relationship and discuss with your partner.

Write a letter to your partner expressing your openness to discussing money matters and your desire to align financial goals. Share your thoughts on how financial compatibility can contribute to long-term relationship success. Reflect on the importance of collaboration and understanding in managing finances as a couple.

Reflect on a time when you and your partner successfully collaborated on a financial decision or goal. Write about the strategies you used to align your priorities and make informed decisions. Reflect on the impact of this collaboration on your relationship and financial well-being.

Lesson 2:

Discussing Money Values and Budgeting

Take turns with your partner and write down three money values that are important to you. Share these writings with each other, focusing on understanding each other's perspectives and discussing areas of alignment or potential differences. Reflect on how these discussions can promote understanding and collaboration in managing finances.

Create a joint budget together, identifying your shared financial goals and priorities. Write down the specific steps you need to take to achieve these goals. Reflect on the benefits of planning and budgeting together in aligning your financial decisions and building a secure and stable relationship.

Write a reflection on a time when financial transparency and trust played a role in resolving a financial conflict or challenge in your relationship. Describe the actions or behaviors that contributed to building trust in financial matters. Reflect on how transparency and trust can strengthen the foundation of your relationship.

Lesson 3:

Seeking Professional Guidance and Support

Write down any financial conflicts or challenges you and your partner have experienced. Reflect on whether seeking professional guidance or support could assist in resolving these issues. If applicable, research and identify resources or professionals that can provide assistance.

Write a letter to a financial advisor or counselor, outlining your financial concerns and questions. Seek their professional guidance on resolving financial conflicts and creating a solid financial plan. Reflect on the potential benefits of seeking external support in managing finances as a couple.

Reflect on the potential impact of financial stress on your relationship. Write down three strategies or actions you can take to reduce financial stress and promote financial well-being. Consider how these strategies can contribute to a more secure and stable relationship.

Chapter 5:
The Writing on the Wall

Lesson 1:

Reflecting on Shared Values and Aspirations

Write a journal entry reflecting on your own values, dreams, and goals for the future. Consider both individual aspirations and those you would like to share with your partner. Reflect on how these values and aspirations contribute to a thriving partnership and a fulfilling life together.

Write a letter to your partner expressing your appreciation for their values, dreams, and goals. Share your thoughts on the importance of aligning your vision for the future. Reflect on how discussing and understanding each other's aspirations can strengthen the bond and create a shared sense of purpose.

Reflect on a time when you and your partner successfully found common ground and made compromises in your long-term plans. Write about the strategies you used to identify and address potential areas of conflict or differences. Reflect on the impact of this collaboration on your relationship and the fulfillment of your shared goals.

Lesson 2:

Reassessing Goals and Priorities

Take turns with your partner and write down three individual goals or priorities that you would like to achieve in the next five years. Share these writings with each other and discuss how they align with your shared vision for the future. Reflect on any potential areas of overlap or conflict and explore possible solutions.

Create a vision board or collage together that represents your shared goals and aspirations. Display it in a visible place as a reminder of your vision and to inspire ongoing commitment. Reflect on the importance of regularly reassessing and updating your goals and priorities to ensure that your relationship stays on track.

Write a reflection on the ways in which your relationship has supported and encouraged your personal growth and development. Describe specific instances or actions that have contributed to your growth. Reflect on how fostering personal growth in each other contributes to the overall success and satisfaction of the relationship.

Lesson 3:

Supporting Each Other's Aspirations

Take turns with your partner and write down three specific ways you can support and encourage each other's personal growth and development. Share these writings with each other and discuss the significance of supporting each other's aspirations. Reflect on the positive impact this support can have on the relationship.

Write a letter to your future self, describing the importance of regularly checking in on your shared values, dreams, and goals. Reflect on specific actions or behaviors you can take to ensure that your relationship remains aligned with your vision for the future. Consider how these efforts can contribute to a fulfilling and thriving partnership.

Reflect on a time when you and your partner faced a challenge or setback in pursuing your shared goals. Write about how you supported each other during that time and how it strengthened your bond. Reflect on the importance of being each other's cheerleader and source of encouragement.

Chapter 6: Room to Grow

Lesson 1:

Exploring Individual Interests and Hobbies

Write a journal entry exploring your individual interests and hobbies. Reflect on how these activities contribute to your personal growth and well-being. Discuss with your partner the importance of nurturing these interests and how they can enhance your relationship.

Take turns with your partner and write down three individual interests or hobbies that you would like to pursue or further develop. Share these writings with each other and discuss how you can support and encourage each other's individual pursuits. Reflect on the positive impact this support can have on your relationship.

Write a reflection on a time when you celebrated and encouraged your partner's personal achievements or pursuits. Describe the emotions and connection you felt during that experience. Reflect on the importance of celebrating each other's individual growth and accomplishments.

Lesson 2:

Establishing Boundaries and Expectations

Take turns with your partner and write down three expectations or boundaries you have regarding personal time and space. Share these writings with each other and discuss how you can honor and respect these boundaries. Reflect on the positive impact of setting clear expectations on promoting understanding and harmony in your relationship.

Write a letter to your future self, outlining your individual goals and aspirations. Reflect on the importance of discussing these goals with your partner and finding ways to support each other's personal growth. Describe specific actions or behaviors you can take to ensure a healthy balance between individual pursuits and shared experiences.

Reflect on a time when you and your partner found a balance between your individual growth and shared experiences. Write about the strategies you used to maintain a sense of togetherness and support while pursuing personal interests. Reflect on how this balance contributes to the vibrancy of your relationship.

Lesson 3:

Creating a Supportive Environment

Take turns with your partner and write down three specific ways you can celebrate and encourage each other's personal achievements and pursuits. Share these writings with each other and discuss how these actions can strengthen your bond. Reflect on the importance of creating a supportive environment that fosters individual growth.

Write a reflection on the importance of balancing individual growth with shared experiences and connections. Describe specific activities or rituals you can incorporate into your relationship to maintain this balance. Reflect on how these efforts contribute to a sense of togetherness and support.

Reflect on a time when you and your partner faced challenges in balancing individual growth and shared experiences. Write about the strategies you used to overcome these challenges and maintain harmony in your relationship. Reflect on the growth and learning that resulted from navigating these experiences together.

Chapter 7: After the Honeymoon

Lesson 1:

Exploring Life Transitions

Write a journal entry reflecting on a significant life transition you and your partner have experienced or anticipate in the future. Describe your expectations, fears, and hopes regarding this transition. Discuss with your partner the importance of open communication and adaptability in navigating these changes.

Take turns with your partner and write down three expectations or concerns you have regarding a specific life transition. Share these writings with each other and engage in a deep conversation about these topics. Reflect on how discussing these expectations, fears, and hopes strengthens your ability to face challenges together.

Write a letter to your future self, reflecting on how you and your partner can foster emotional attunement and support during times of transition. Describe specific actions or behaviors you can take to create a supportive environment. Reflect on the significance of emotional support in strengthening the relationship during these periods.

Lesson 2:

Creating New Rituals and Traditions

Take turns with your partner and write down three ideas for new rituals, traditions, or shared experiences that can help navigate and thrive during life transitions. Share these writings with each other and discuss the potential impact of these ideas on your relationship. Reflect on the importance of creating new experiences that bring you closer together during times of change.

Write a reflection on a time when you and your partner successfully created a new ritual or tradition during a life transition. Describe the impact of this ritual or tradition on your relationship and how it helped you navigate the change. Reflect on the importance of being intentional about creating meaningful shared experiences.

Reflect on the concept of lifelong learning and growth as a couple. Write about specific areas or skills you and your partner would like to explore or develop together. Reflect on how embracing lifelong learning and growth allows for continued evolution and renewal in your relationship.

Lesson 3:

Planning for Life Transitions

Take turns with your partner and write down three action steps you can take to prepare for an anticipated life transition. Share these writings with each other and discuss the importance of proactive planning. Reflect on how these action steps can help you navigate the transition with greater ease and resilience.

Write a reflection on the importance of adaptability in times of change. Describe a specific instance when you and your partner demonstrated adaptability during a life transition. Reflect on the lessons learned and how they can be applied to future transitions. Discuss with your partner the value of being flexible and open-minded during these periods.

Reflect on the concept of renewal and growth in your relationship. Write about specific actions or behaviors you can take to foster ongoing evolution as a couple. Reflect on the potential benefits of embracing change and growth together.

Chapter 8: Let Love Rule

Lesson 1:

Cultivating Appreciation and Kindness

Take turns with your partner and write down three specific ways you can cultivate appreciation, kindness, and generosity in your relationship. Share these writings with each other and discuss how these actions can foster love and connection. Reflect on the impact of expressing appreciation and kindness on the overall atmosphere of your relationship.

Write a journal entry expressing gratitude for your partner. Reflect on their positive qualities, gestures, and actions that you appreciate. Share your entry with your partner and discuss how gratitude can deepen the emotional bond between you. Reflect on the importance of practicing gratitude regularly.

Reflect on a time when you and your partner experienced kindness or generosity from each other. Write about the emotions and connection you felt during that experience. Describe how you can create opportunities to be kind and generous in your relationship. Discuss with your partner the importance of fostering a culture of kindness and generosity.

Lesson 2:

Expressing Love and Affection

Take turns with your partner and write down three specific ways you can express love and affection in meaningful ways. Share these writings with each other and discuss how these expressions can strengthen the emotional bond between you. Reflect on the importance of intentional acts of love and affection in your relationship.

Write a love letter or a heartfelt message to your partner. Express your love, admiration, and appreciation. Share your letter with your partner and discuss the impact of such expressions on your relationship. Reflect on the power of verbal and written affirmations of love and affection.

Reflect on a time when you and your partner experienced a particularly meaningful expression of love or affection. Write about the impact of that experience on your connection. Describe specific actions or behaviors you can engage in to continue nurturing love and affection in your relationship.

Lesson 3:

Practicing Forgiveness and Letting Go

Take turns with your partner and write down three instances where you can practice forgiveness and let go of past hurts. Share these writings with each other and discuss how forgiveness can allow you to move forward and build a resilient relationship. Reflect on the power of forgiveness in promoting healing and growth.

Write a letter to yourself, reflecting on the importance of forgiveness in your relationship. Describe a specific situation where you forgave your partner or were forgiven by them. Share your letter with your partner and discuss the significance of forgiveness in nurturing love and connection. Reflect on how forgiveness contributes to a healthier and happier relationship.

Reflect on the concept of letting go of past hurts. Write about specific actions or strategies you can use to release resentment and embrace forgiveness. Discuss with your partner the importance of addressing past hurts and working towards a future filled with love and understanding.

Made in United States
Troutdale, OR
03/18/2025